Anthony White

FROM hOBBY to moNey

THE ESSENTIAL GUIDE FOR CONVERTING YOUR SKILLS AND PASSION INTO A BUSINESS.

FROM HOBBY

TO MONEY

The essential guide for converting your skills and

passion into a business.

Anthony White

COPYRIGHT

DEDICATION

I would like to dedicate this book to every person who

wants to earn more and enjoy while they earn.

Table of Contents

PROLOGUE

I gave James, my eight-year-old nephew, a freshly knit jumper as a gift. "Thank you so much, Aunt Sophie, this is far better than the expensive sweater my mom got for us last week," he said in response.

James hastened off after his kind acceptance of my present, but I lingered, wondering if my work was indeed excellent enough to be sold.

"I was aware that young people are fairly candid in their reviews.

Yes! I assured myself that I am competent. This was the last push I required to convert my pastime into a source of revenue.

-Sophie, Dallas, Tx.

Maybe a lot of you are like Sophie, unsure of your abilities or of what to do with your talents. I'm here to tell you that it can bring you a respectable income and, beyond that, make a difference in your community.

Join me on this journey as we learn exactly how to do it

in **FROM HOBBY TO MONEY**

CHAPTER 1

Finding the right hobby

The finest thing about a hobby is that you can't do any pretending about it. You either like it or you don't.

– Dorothy Draper

When choosing a hobby, the first thing to consider is the personality type. The response to this question will affect the kinds of things you normally draw toward.

The "Big 5" personality qualities are the five basic dimensions of personality, according to many modern personality psychologists.

Extraversion (often known as extroversion), agreeableness, openness, conscientiousness, and neuroticism are the 5 major personality qualities.

Conscientiousness is thinking, openness is intrigue and creativity, extraversion is sociability, agreeableness is friendliness, openness is creativity, and neuroticism is typically associated with melancholy or emotional instability.

Without taking a personality traits exam, you can delve deeper into your own personality by understanding each personality trait and what it means to score well or poorly in that trait.

Based on where they are on the spectrum for each of the personality qualities described, it can also assist you in comprehending others better.

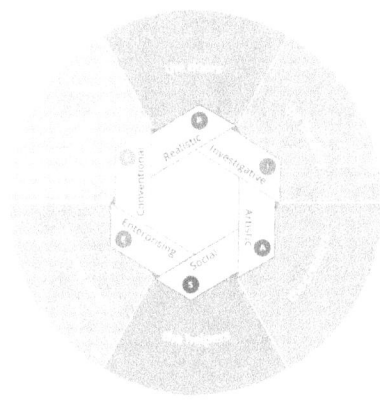

Myer-Briggs Personality Wheel Source: The Myer-Briggs Company

How Personality Affects Interest

It is well established that some character traits prefer to excel at particular interests.

For instance, organized people can indeed be good auditors, stamp collectors, and antique dealers.

People with an artistic tendency can pursue hobbies like writing, drawing, and singing. If you're extroverted, you might want to try rock climbing, hiking, or becoming a volunteer tour guide for visitors to your city.

It all starts with an in-depth examination of your identity, followed by a consideration of your preferences.

For instance, I've always had a creative and analytical mind, so when I found chess, I was hooked straight away. Chess became both a way to relax and a method for me to develop my ability to think critically.

Here's a short step by step guide;

Make a choice, give it some thought, and do some research.

Spend some time considering what you enjoy doing before deciding what you're looking for in a hobby. What are some of the things you love doing? What are some of the things you excel at?

Some people like sports or active hobbies like hiking. Others favor more sedentary pursuits like reading or handicraft. There is no right or wrong answer, so it's important to pick a hobby that suits your personality.

You can begin narrowing your possibilities once you have a broad notion of the kind of hobby you're interested in.

Be explicit about what you're searching for while choosing a hobby because there are countless options available. Let's say you want to start a career in design. In that scenario, you have to choose if you want to spend significant time studying graphic or web design. You could also want to make stunning thumbnails and images. It's time to start your investigation after deciding on the basic category of hobby you're interested in. Consult with loved ones and friends who have similar interests. Read books and articles on the subject of your preferred activity. Finding the ideal activity will be easier the more you understand it.

Obtain feedback from relatives and friends.

Finding a passion that suits your personality might be helped by asking your friends and family for suggestions because they are familiar with you.

They can make suggestions for things you might like. Another benefit is that they may offer advice and encouragement as you experiment with new interests.

Engage in a few various hobbies.

A fantastic method to discover a hobby you like is to try out a few different ones. Whether you are extroverted or creative or if you are more introverted, numerous choices abound. You might want to try something physical. You have countless options, so don't be scared to try different things until you find something you like.

As you participate in the hobby, pay attention to your emotions. You can use it to decide if the pastime is a good fit for you. It's probably a good fit if you discover that you're enjoying the pastime and it's not stressing you out. The same goes if you experience tension or boredom while engaging in the hobby.

Verify the cost of the hobby.

There are some things to think about. First, it's crucial to be truthful about the costs of the pastime you choose. Do your homework in advance to determine what you will need to get started and what it will cost. Let's say you want to learn how to paint. If so, attempt to learn how much the paints and other supplies will cost, as well as how much any classes or lessons you might wish to take will cost.

It's also critical to think about your ability to sustain your new pastime in the long run. Consider the expense of boarding, lessons, and veterinarian fees if you ride horses, for instance. The only costs you will need to think about, though, are the initial purchase of supplies if your passion is knitting.

Consider whether your new pastime has any potential for

financial gain. Even if it's not a deal-breaker, it can be beneficial to think about whether your activity might someday generate revenue.

Don't be afraid to change hobbies if you're not enjoying them. If you're not enjoying your interests, there's nothing wrong with switching them. In this situation, it might even be a good idea to switch interests. Talk to folks who like the same activities as you or who have different interests. They might be able to recommend some worthwhile new hobbies to try.

Enjoy yourself and your new passion!

It's crucial to appreciate your new pastime because it should be enjoyable. There are a few techniques to ensure that your new hobby is enjoyable:

Create reasonable expectations

Some hobbies can take a while to get the hang of. Stick with it, and don't get discouraged if you don't get it right away.

Be imaginative.

Don't be scared to add your own unique spin to hobbies because many of them are up to interpretation.

People should know about your activity. Sharing your pastime with people who have similar interests to yours is one of the finest ways to appreciate it. Either in person or online are options.

You're setting yourself up for disappointment if you expect to become an expert at your new activity over night. Enjoy the learning process and take your time. Be tolerant!

CHAPTER 2

Upskilling

"Learning never exhausts the mind."
— Leonardo da Vinci

An employee's talents are expanded and skill gaps are reduced through training programs and professional development opportunities offered as part of the upskilling trend, which promotes continual learning in the workplace. Upskilling concentrates on enhancing the skill sets of present employees, typically through training, so they can progress in their professions and discover new roles and possibilities within the organization.

Although it is frequently employed in the job, upskilling is crucial for turning a pastime into money.

Having faith in your ability to sell your work is one of the hardest challenges. This lack of assurance might cause work to be priced below its true worth or prevent it from being released onto the market.

Upskilling is a way to improve your craft confidence and skill assurance. A key strategy for transforming a pastime into a craft is this. Consider the knowledge and abilities you'll need to advance from enthusiast to professional status.

Several methods for upskilling include:

Microlearning; mentorship and shadowing; "lunch and learn" meetings; and virtual or online courses.

In my time as a consultant, I have met a couple of people who have been able to turn hobby to money, here are some stories.

Case Study 1: Nail Garden

Grace first became interested in nail art when she was a college student. She made the decision to pursue it as a pastime and began with her own nails.

She had to clean it up before anyone inquired who had done the terrible job on her hands when the art didn't turn out perfectly. She still took great pleasure in it all.

Finally, she made the decision to actually study nail art. She spent a lot of time, money, and effort on it.

She completed a 3-month apprenticeship, and because of her prior expertise, she was able to catch up quickly.

She now owns Nail Garden, a nail salon where customers may receive the greatest nail care. She was able to make money from her pastime.

Case Study 2: El Gibbor Soap

Mrs. Sherry has always put her community first. Sharing her soap for free, people eventually started praising the soap's caliber. She created it to the highest grade possible as opposed to the ordinary ones, which were greatly diluted, because she wanted to offer them a decent gift.

By enrolling in an online course on producing high-quality liquid soap, Mrs. Sherry decided to upgrade her skills. She eventually mastered the art of creating various soaps for washing, bathing, etc.

She now operates a small business from her house and provides her neighborhood with reasonably priced, high-quality soaps.

Case Study 3: Bluprint Digital

Chris began drawing at the age of 2 and kept doing so all the way through college. Although he was an engineering student, he continued to like art. Just before graduation, Chris received encouragement from a friend to pursue his passion for drawing. After some soul-searching, he decided to pursue his studies in drawing and graphics design. He struggled for nearly six months to master the concepts and methods, but he was committed to improving

his skills. Three years later, Chris is an accomplished creative director and graphic designer who owns and operates his own advertising company. He was able to develop his pastime into a job and, eventually, a company.

Case study 4: Max teaches chess

Max is the type of person who seems to be good at everything, but chess has always remained with him. He made the decision to push things even farther by joining a chess club, reading a ton of books, taking part in both online and offline competitions, and joining a club.

Max eventually developed into a strong club player and took home a few regional titles. He considered how to make money from his pastime and started Max teaches chess, a course that introduces schoolchildren and chess novices to the game's fundamentals.

He also offers a course for players who want to advance from being amateurs to strong club players.

The wonderful thing is that he also works as a business analyst, so he doesn't do this full-time. In conclusion, he made money from his hobby.

These individuals are some of the case studies that show how to get money from hobbies. There is a quick task left that you should finish in at least an hour.

Important Questions to Answer

- What skills are needed to become a pro in my chosen hobby.

- How can I acquire those skills

- How can I translate those skills to income

- What emerging technology is applicable to the chosen hobby?

- How profitable is this hobby if I upskill?

Page Left Blank

CHAPTER 3

Starting a Small Business

"The beginning is always today."
– Mary Wollstonecraft Shelley

Generally speaking, a small business is a privately held corporation, partnership, or sole proprietorship with fewer employees and lower yearly income than a corporation or regular-sized business. In terms of being eligible for government assistance and advantageous tax treatment, the meaning of "small" differs by nation and sector. According to a set of criteria based on particular industries, the U.S. Small Business Administration determines what constitutes a small business.

Industry	Not to exceed
Manufacturing and mining	500 employees
Wholesale trade	100 employees
Retail and service	$6 million average annual revenue
General and heavy construction	$28.5 million average annual revenue
Special trade contractors	$12 million average annual revenue
Agriculture	$0.75 million average annual revenue

Source: https://asq.org/quality-resources/small-business

A new business is like a baby being welcomed into the world. There is a stage of pregnancy where we feel pain but cannot physically see anything, yet we are aware that something is on the way.

This is the time when we mull over concepts, conduct market research, secure money, etc.

The delivery phase comes next; this is when we venture into the unknown. However, many people remain pregnant their entire lives without ever giving birth to their dreams, because it takes a lot of force. Don't be that way; give birth to your dreams by going through labor.

Then there is the weaning stage, where patience is needed, a lot of care must be given to the business, and you shouldn't have high expectations (just like you wouldn't!) for a newborn.

Following weaning, the baby develops and starts to grow, taking care of you and other people.

At this point, we start to see revenue and significant influence.

Let's divide this up into more steps;

Stage 1 (pregnancy):

Develop your concept.

You most certainly already have a concept of what you want to sell online, or at the very least, the market you want to join, if you're thinking about launching a business. Look up existing businesses in the industry you've chosen. Discover how you can improve what you're doing by studying what the current market leaders are doing. You have a good idea and are prepared to write a business plan if you believe your company can offer something that other businesses can't (or can do the same thing, but more quickly and cheaply).

Define your "why?"

Plan your business.

You may handle important areas of the firm more clearly by using a business plan. It contains everything, including your financials and executive summary.

By jumping into things without thinking them through, inexperienced business entrepreneurs might make a lot of mistakes. You must identify your ideal clientele. Who will purchase your good or service? If you can't uncover any indication that there is a market for your idea, what would be the point?

Name-drop ideas for your company.

Whichever solution you select, it's critical to comprehend the justification for your notion. As a precautionary measure, avoid creating a business plan or generating ideas

for a company name before determining the idea's worth.

Make a financial assessment.

It requires money to start a business, therefore you must decide how you will pay for it. Will you need to borrow money or do you have the resources to finance your startup? Do you have enough savings to go by till you turn a profit if you intend to quit your job to concentrate on your business? Identify the beginning fees that you will incur.

Because they run out of money before making a profit, many startups fail. It's never a bad idea to anticipate your startup costs because it may take some time before the company starts to generate stable income.

Stage 2 (Birth Stage):

Register your company

You will typically need to formally register your business. To dispel any uncertainties, check with your local government body.

Several instances of legal structures are;

Sole proprietorship: If you intend to be solely liable for all debts and responsibilities and independently control the firm, you may choose to register as a sole proprietorship. Be advised that taking this path may negatively impact your credit.

Partnership: A business partnership, as its name suggests, is one in which two or more people are jointly and severally liable as the company's owners. If you can locate a business partner with abilities that compliment your own, you don't have to struggle on your own. If you want your business to be successful, adding someone to the mix usually makes sense.

Corporation: Before considering whether to separate your personal liability from that of your company, consider the advantages and disadvantages.

Despite the fact that each type of corporation is subject to a particular set of rules, this legal framework often creates a business that is distinct from its owners. As a result, companies have the same legal rights as people to own property, bear responsibility, pay taxes, enter into contracts, and bring legal actions. According to Deryck Jordan, managing attorney of Jordan Counsel, "Companies, especially C corporations, are especially ideal for young enterprises that plan on "coming public" or seeking money from venture capitalists.

Limited liability company: The limited liability company is one of the most popular business structures for small enterprises (LLC). This hybrid organization offers the tax advantages of a partnership as well as the legal protections

of a corporation.

Determine your Brand Identity

Your brand identity will be determined by your business approach. This will determine things like your logo, brand colors, typefaces, graphics, communication, etc.

To help with this crucial stage, a competent graphic designer and a brand strategist should be consulted. Because consumers engage with businesses as though they were people, it is necessary to build a distinct brand archetype (brand personality) at this point.

In the chapter about building a brand, this topic will be covered in more detail.

Build your team

To launch your business, you'll need to assemble a fantastic team, unless you intend to be its sole employee. Having a team, no matter how tiny, is crucial.

These people could be suppliers, consultants, accountability partners, employees (if necessary), or even volunteers. Some firms are founded by volunteers who trade labor for experience in the field. This is a beneficial technique to give back while obtaining inexpensive labor to launch your company.

People create your stuff, declared Zawadzki. Finding your founding team, figuring out any gaps, and deciding how and when to fill them should be your top priorities.

Equally crucial is figuring out how the team will function as a whole. You'll avoid a lot of problems later on if you define roles and responsibilities, the division of labor, how to provide feedback, and how to collaborate when everyone is not in the same room.

Stage 3 (Growth Stage)

Market yourself more vigorously.

You should devote more time and money to advertising now that your company is up and operating. How many people are unaware that your product even exists will surprise you.

You must also be the brand's loudest spokesperson.

Excellent customer service

This is essential to the success of your company. Make sure you receive reviews frequently.

Also improve your client interaction.

Perhaps the best source of fresh leads and potential clients comes from their recommendations. If you have workers, make sure they receive frequent training on how to provide better customer service.

Make research and development investments

Upskilling is ongoing for both you, the business owner, and your employees (if any). To make sure you stay on top of advancements in that industry, a concentrated effort must be made.

Keep an eye on your finances.

You must monitor your finances carefully. Although for many small firms, this doesn't require employing a specialist.

I'll give you some tips on how to make sure you have a

firm hold on your cash flow in the following chapter.

Page Left Blank

CHAPTER 4

Financial recording for small businesses

"Balancing your money is the key to having enough."

– Elizabeth Warren Amelia Warren Tyagin

Everywhere there are small business owners, recordkeeping is a critical and occasionally challenging aspect of making sure a business runs properly. Keeping accurate records of earnings, expenses, payroll, taxes, and accounts is not merely wise financial management. It can ease your mind, aid in goal monitoring, and help you save time and money.

Simply put, financial record-keeping involves keeping track of all of your company's financial activities, such as tracking sales, inputting vendor invoices, and processing payroll. Basically, you will be keeping track of every transaction that involves money entering or leaving your bank account.

Creating your own "free" spreadsheet system to keep track of all business transactions is popular in the early stages of business ownership, but it may be time-consuming, labor-intensive, and ineffective. However, even the most basic accounting software will make it easier to keep track of all your company's activities and is a wise investment.

Knowing what kinds of records you should preserve is crucial whether you are manually creating an Excel spreadsheet or using accounting software. You should retain all receipts that will support your running costs, gross sales receipts, and vendor purchases in order to properly track your business operations.

No matter who maintains the accounts and records for your company, it is crucial to comprehend the following four fundamental documents/reports:

Income Statement: This document displays the profitability of your company as well as any profits or losses for any specific time period.

Balance Sheet: A balance sheet gives a summary of the financial position of your company at a specific point in time The balance sheet also displays the company's retaining earnings, or the amount of profit that has been put back into the company rather than dispersed to owners.

Cash Flow Statement: Analyses the operating, finance, and investment activities of your company to demonstrate how much money is coming in and going out. The cash flow statement differs from an income statement in that it does not include non-cash expenses like depreciation and monitors money borrowed on a note payable or spent on assets.

Bank Reconciliation: Compares the transactions you've recorded in your bank account to those you've recorded in the general ledger or book (this is the process of reconciling your book balance to your bank balance)

Basic records include:

- Business expenses

- Sales records

- Accounts receivable

- Accounts payable

- Customer list

- Vendors

- Employee information

- Tax documents

- Invoices

- Purchase orders

- Receipts

- Banks statements

- Contracts

Keeping these records will help you:

1. Be aware of the financial commitment required to produce your good or service.

2. Get a good insight into pricing

3. Evaluate budgeted amounts against actual expenses

4. Monitor spending

5. Select wisely when making purchases

6. Get ready for tax season

7. Easily have access to staff and customer information

8. Guard your company against audits and personnel problems.

9. Estimate estimated revenue

10. Keep track of all money transactions.

Now that you've chosen a bookkeeping system and established your set of financial accounts, it's time to keep track of how your money is actually being used. In addition to having the necessary information on hand, you must choose which accounts will be credited and debited.

Imagine, for instance, that you have recently invested in a new point-of-sale system for your retail company. The system cost you $2,000 and was paid for in cash. Two accounts will be impacted by the transaction: cash (an asset account) and equipment (also an asset). You would record a $2,000 debit (on the left) for the equipment account and a $2,000 credit (on the right) for the cash account since your cash is decreasing while your equipment is increasing.

Always make sure that every debit and credit transaction is properly documented in the appropriate account. Otherwise, your account balances won't match, making it impossible for you to determine the true financial state of your company.

The majority of accounting programs will automatically import your bank information, saving you the time and effort of manually entering and organizing each transaction. If you're using spreadsheet software as your GL, you'll need to enter each transaction by hand.

Close the books.

Balancing and closing the books is the final stage in fundamental bookkeeping. The totals should line up when you add up account debits and credits—often at the end of the day, week, month, quarter, and year. If they do, your books are "balanced" as a result.

As debits and credits, you have been logging journal entries to accounts. You'll "publish" these transactions to the accounts in the general ledger at the end of the period to update the account balances. For example, if over the course of the month your cash account has had $3,000 in debits (increases) and $5,000 in credits (decreases), you would adjust the cash account balance by a total of $2,000 (as a decrease).

Follow this method to adjust the balances for each account in your ledger. At the end of this process, you'll have what's called an "adjusted trial balance." When you combine accounts types, the adjusted balances should meet the accounting equation:

Assets = Liabilities + Equity

You will need to go back and look for problems in the ledger and journal entries if two sides of the equations don't match. Continue the process until the accounts are balanced, then enter any necessary corrections in the journal and ledger. Once that is done, you can close the books and create financial reports.

Once more, the majority of this procedure is handled automatically by accounting software, including the creation of the financial reports we'll cover next.

Prepare financial reports

You must examine the meaning of your books more closely now that you have balanced your books. An overview of the cash flow in each account paints a picture of the financial stability of your business. Then, you may utilize that image to guide future decisions for your company.

Some of the most typical financial reports produced in bookkeeping are listed below:

Balance sheet: This document provides a snapshot of the assets, liabilities, and equity of your company at a certain point in time. Your assets should be equal to the total of your obligations plus equity. The balance sheet offers a glance at the current condition of your company and shows if it can grow or whether it has to set aside cash.

Profit and loss (P&L) statement: This report, which is also known as an income statement, provides a timeline of the company's revenues, costs, and expenses (e.g., quarter). You can analyse your revenues and expenses on the P&L and create projections.

Cash flow statement: Similar to the P&L, the statement of cash flow excludes any non-cash expenses like depreciation. Cash flow statements provide information on your company's revenue, expenses, short-term viability, and ability to cover its debts.

You may create several of these financial reports in real-time with the use of bookkeeping software.

For small-business owners who must make prompt financial decisions based on the current condition of their company, this can be a lifesaver.

Page left Blank

CHAPTER 5

Building a Brand

"A brand for a company is like a
reputation for a person. You earn
reputation by trying to do hard
things well."

– Jeff Bezos

Building your brand.

The business world is a personality-driven environment. This is particularly true of brand voice, or how a corporation communicates through text, audio, and other media. A distinct brand voice is essential to forging better ties with both existing and potential clients.

Your brand voice has the ability to communicate to the world who you are, what you stand for, and what you're aiming to achieve when employed effectively. You just need to express it in words.

What are brand guidelines?

A brand style guide, often known as brand guidelines, is essentially a how-to guide for communicating your brand.

In addition to vital information about a company's voice,

tone, and messaging, they set out all the visual aspects. They come in the form of a booklet, either printed or digital, that contains illustrations of appropriate and inappropriate behavior.

Brand standards address every aspect of a company's identification, such as its:

Full logos, supplemental logos, and icons

Primary and secondary color schemes

Font sizes, styles, and spacing in typography

Other images include photographs, drawings, and artwork.

How a brand employs language and emotion depends on its voice and tone.

How to create your brand voice

Decide who you are.

It's fantastic if you already know who you are as a brand, but it's also fine if you don't. It's only time to conduct some introspection on the business level.

Finding out who you are as a brand and who you aspire to be can be accomplished by asking yourself some more introspective questions. Asking yourself the following questions can help you define your brand identity.

- What three words, if any, would you use to sum up your business?

- What do I hope to be renowned for in the industry?

- What are the main aims and principles of my business?

- What kind of change would I like to see in my sector?

Your ability to incorporate your identity into your branding will increase as you get greater clarity about who you are and what you stand for. As a consequence, your brand will stand out and attract clients' attention.

Keep your target market in mind

Regardless matter what they sell, every brand needs to have a target audience. Do some in-depth research on the consumers of your brand (or develop personas if your business isn't yet operational).

Follow these guidelines:

Obtain accurate statistics: On demographics and average ages. This will assist you in developing more specific parameters for the framework of your brand voice. After all, speaking to millennials is not likely to be the same as speaking to Gen Z or Gen Alpha.

Look at your rivals: How do they communicate with their clients?

Request immediate feedback:

When prompted, about one in three people give feedback, and 77% of consumers are more inclined to favor your brand as a result.

Conduct thorough A/B testing on written material:

How do consumers react differently to commercials featuring emojis versus those without?

A brand voice's success totally depends on the data collection procedure. Take a few months to get oriented; don't rush or cut corners.

Create a brand archetype.

Even though there are countless distinct brand voices in use today, the most of them are just rehashed stereotypes. These are referred to as "brand archetypes" in general.

The personality characteristics known as brand archetypes have been around for thousands of years, and are almost the same irrespective of culture or language, instantly identifiable. This is why brand archetypes can make it easier for audiences to relate to brands and the ideas they're trying to convey.

Knowing your archetype is crucial to success because 77% of consumers engage with brands that share their values. Choosing a brand archetype (or a combination of archetypes) will assist in generating more specific ideas regarding the tone that your brand should adopt. For instance: Disney, Lego, and other companies with the Magician archetype rely heavily on playful, imaginative, and comforting language.

Companies like Dollar Shave Club, Old Spice, and M&Ms that fit the Jester archetype place a strong emphasis on witty, humorous, or outlandish language.

The majority of luxury companies that fit the Ruler archetype (Rolex, Lamborghini, and Gucci) place an emphasis on forceful, matter-of-fact brand voices.

Spend some time getting to know your brand's archetype. Feel free to combine and contrast to create a tone that works for your business.

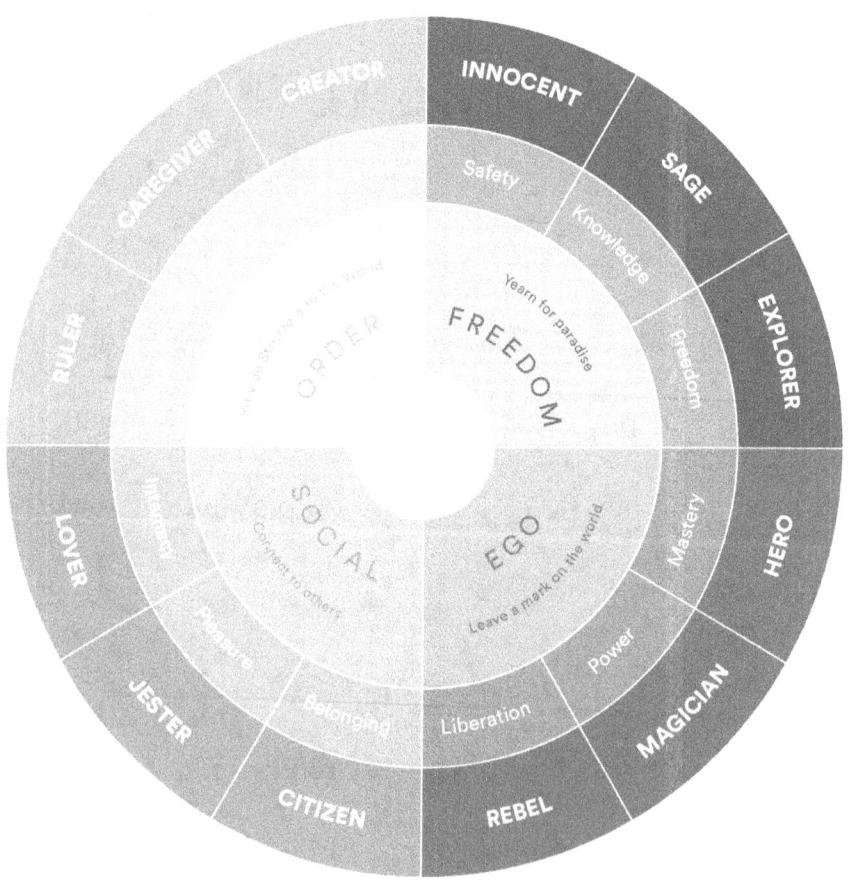

From hobby to money

CHAPTER 6

Getting word out (Marketing & Sales)

"Ignoring online marketing is like opening a business but not telling anyone."

– KB Marketing Agency

Getting and keeping customers is the goal of marketing for small businesses. It is described as the procedure a business uses to market, sell, and distribute a good or service. Businesses can develop customer interest through marketing, then capitalize on that enthusiasm to increase sales. Effective marketing is a necessity for all organizations, no matter how big or little, if they want to expand and succeed.

The goal of marketing is to make sure that your customers are aware of the important aspects of your company, such as: Who you are as a company, what your products and services are, what sets you apart from the competition, what needs of your customers you are addressing, and why they should buy from you.

Building on the data gathered during your market research initiatives is marketing. You ought to be able to identify your target market and determine your niche based on your research. Having an understanding of their needs and preferences. You should also be informed of your competitors' products, pricing, and distribution methods. This information assists you in creating a marketing strategy that is tailored to your target market and sets you apart from the competition.

The Four Questions to Ask

Analyzing four crucial aspects that affect the purchasing decision can be beneficial when deciding on the best strategy to sell your company. The four Ps of marketing are these elements:

What are you going to market as a product?

Price: What will you be charging for your product?

Location: Where will people buy your product?

How are you going to spread the word about your product?

These elements can be included in a marketing plan, which can be included in a broader business plan or used as a standalone document. Your strategy should include a comprehensive promotional calendar that lists all of your marketing initiatives along with their respective prices. When beginning a new firm, many entrepreneurs underestimate the cost of marketing, especially during the initial stages.

Marketing Suggestions for New Businesses

Make sure your contact information is legible and that your business cards include a description of your goods and services before investing in them (use the back of the card) Utilize free or inexpensive marketing tools like networking groups, social media, regional business directories, press releases about your company, event sponsorships for neighborhood nonprofits, etc.

Create a compelling elevator pitch, this is a succinct 30–60 second introduction to your company, products, or services. You may make your pitch more memorable by including an intriguing personal or business fact or story.

Request recommendations and testimonials from your current clients.

Think about implementing incentive schemes to promote repeat business

You can promote your company to customers in a variety of ways. Your advertising strategy and message are critical to attracting customers and generating sales.

Marketing is a continuous business activity that must change along with your company, your clients, and the market.

Digital marketing

Social Media Marketing

For a brand or company, social media marketing is now an absolute must. When it comes to engaging, influencing, and converting, social networks are where you want to be because there are so many different demographics using them globally.

Look at these figures from the Digital 2022: Global Overview Report to understand why:

Nearly 60% of the world's population—4.6 billion individuals—are engaged social media users.

2.27 hours are typically spent daily on social media.

The number of TikTok, YouTube, and Instagram users has increased.

Every month, people use 7.5 platforms on average.

The following steps will help you develop a successful social media strategy:

1. Establish business objectives, such as those related to signups, awareness, clicks, transactions, etc.

2. Conduct content research and develop a content calendar that is in line with this objective. Do you plan to create videos, cards, lifestyle stuff, etc.? A family member or professional with knowledge of current social media trends, content creation, and visual design may be needed for this.

3. Choose the social media network or platforms that will work best for your brand. This can involve some trial and error.

The world of digital marketing is dynamic and ever-changing. Its rapid evolution over the previous two years has been demonstrated. Although there have been a number of new marketing trends, it might not be feasible for your small business to implement all of these marketing techniques.

You might be hesitant to try some of the daring marketing trends because of your restricted funds and resources. Having said that, we can say with confidence that you have access to a variety of marketing techniques that will help you develop your brand and expand your small business.

The seven small business marketing tactics that can produce outstanding results are covered below.

1. Customized email advertising

Customers want for individualized attention, and email marketing offers the ideal remedy. Email marketing is a popular approach for customer acquisition and retention because it is one of the most popular marketing strategies for small businesses.

Personalized emails help you connect with your customers on a deeper level. To nurture leads at different stages and make their buying experience as joyful as possible, drip email campaigns using email list management software can be used.

Your brand appears more real to customers when emails are customized. By going one step further with personalization, you may create special offers and coupons for your devoted consumers based on their past purchases and preferences.

2. Automated marketing

Many of your business operations can be streamlined with the aid of automation. To save time and increase employee productivity, it is crucial for small businesses to automate their marketing procedures. One of the essential marketing tactics for your company if you want to operate wisely and expand is automation.

There are excellent automation solutions for lead scoring and nurturing, systematic content, and email marketing. publishing, social media administration, referral advertising, and many other things. In addition to increasing team productivity, automation can dramatically increase conversion rates.

3. Brand story

The days of aggressive sales are over. Telling a story is the key to marketing your goods and services. With a fresh perspective, content marketing is still one of the greatest marketing techniques for small businesses.

Invest in developing personalized content rather than bragging to your target markct about how great your product is. Tell potential customers how your product has aided in your customers' resolution of a specific issue.

Has your product facilitated your consumers' quicker achievement of a given objective? Present it with statistics and examples from the real world. Top tools like Yoast seo can help you improve the SEO value of your content.

4. Use of influencers

Did you believe that the bigger brands were the only ones who benefited from influencer marketing?

That is not true. One of the effective marketing techniques for a small business to increase brand recognition and produce high-quality leads is influencer marketing.

On social media sites like Instagram and TikTok, influencers have their own devoted fan bases that engage with them and look to them for advice. This is one of the greatest marketing tactics for your small business because it has a high engagement rate. You can choose and enter into an agreement with influencers operating in your niche and area to authentically promote your business.

If your company is centered on the plant-based movement, you may want to collaborate with influencers who support a vegan or dairy-free diet. You can get in touch with a target audience with a lot of potential for minimal financial outlay.

5. Listing on Google My Business

Every small business that wants to improve its internet visibility must have a Google My Business (GMB) listing.

Why is it necessary?

Google searches reveal that individuals visit 1.5 billion

locations each month, and 76% of those who look for something nearby visit the business within a day.

It is essential that you endeavor to establish a robust online presence for your business so that potential clients may find you when they search online.

Your company can gain the extensive visibility and reputation it needs by adding a listing to Google My Business.

As a result, it ought to rank among your small business's top marketing strategies.

6. Online event promotion

Digital events have become increasingly popular in recent years. Podcasts, online conferences, live chats, and webinars are effective methods for organizations to produce high-quality leads online.

Additionally, these online events give brands the chance to learn more about their audiences and promote to them directly.

As a small business owner, you can participate in or organize online events to introduce your offerings and the problems they solve to your target market. By interacting with your customers through surveys and polls, you may also learn more about their preferences and adjust your marketing tactics accordingly.

7. Marketing by referral

Utilizing different kinds of referral programs to capitalize on a happy customer's goodwill is one of the best marketing methods for small businesses. Ask your customers to tell their friends and family about the things they love when they are satisfied with your brand.

Take the food sector as an example. If you can learn to please clients who value comfort and convenience, your chances of getting their recommendations to their contacts increase. You can politely encourage these clients to tell their friends about your goods and reward them for sending you quality prospects.

Making decisions about your small-business marketing plans

Because your company is distinct, so too should your marketing tactics be. You shouldn't, however, lose sight of the fact that some small businesses still find value in and relevance to more traditional marketing techniques like fliers and posters.

These digital marketing techniques, which range from using automated tools and local SEO to referral marketing, can help your small business expand. Try them out to help your business succeed.

Page left Blank

CHAPTER 6

Scaling your business

"You don't build a business, you build people, then people build the business."

– Zig Ziglar

A scaling business model is successful when it enables a company to grow at a rate equal to its costs, increasing its profitability as it expands. In contrast, a non-scalable business must develop at a rate far faster than its costs in order to be profitable. Non-scalable businesses have large costs as they expand.

Professional service organizations like consulting and law frequently use scaling business models. In these kinds of enterprises, a company's revenue is directly inversely correlated with the number of customers it has. As a result, it is a scalable business because growing the clientele generates growing earnings.

If you want to determine whether a business model is scalable, you should consider how many customers it requires to make a profit and whether growing revenue generates new customers. Growth stages, income, and expenses are some additional important factors to take into account when figuring out whether a business strategy is scalable.

Various business growth stages have an impact on a business model's ability to scale. For instance, a business may not have the necessary infrastructure to enable rapid expansion during the beginning phase because it is usually focused on revenue-generating tactics and growth plans. As a result, once a business has beyond the initial stages of growth, it is crucial to think about how it will continue to scale.

When deciding if a business strategy is scalable, revenue is still another crucial aspect to take into account. A business with high sales but low profit margins might not be able to scale as quickly as one with lower revenue but greater profit margins. This is so that the later company can invest more in growth, whilst the former must reinvest its profits back into the company to sustain its existing rate of growth.

Finally, costs must also be taken into account when figuring out whether a business model is scalable. A business may not be able to scale as quickly as another if it has higher fixed costs (like rent or salaries). This is due to the fact that the latter will be able to use its excess money to invest in growth, but the former would have to create income exponentially to cover its increasing expenses.

Here are the top 10 advices for growing your company.

1. Developing a Strong Skill Set

It is obvious that scaling requires a broader skill set. Entrepreneurs must assemble a group of people with a variety of skills. It's critical that your staff comprehends your business objectives and works diligently to meet them on time without compromising on quality. They must possess an exceptional skill set in order for it to be achievable.

Invest in your team, if necessary, as their growth will ultimately lessen your workload and enable you to scale your business successfully.

2. Collaboration and Networking

The mindset that encourages expansion and scalability must include external relationships and cooperation. The secret to long-term success is building a strong PR network.

One of the best business coaches in India advises that you create a network of partnerships with individuals and groups, such as service providers, sales partners, suppliers, and customers, as they may be willing to help you by offering crucial market information. Scalability becomes easily attainable when such engagements take the shape of a formal alliance, which may happen.

3. **Purchasing technology**

Technology helps business owners scale their operations more easily and affordably. If you strategically spend your time and money on technology, you can achieve huge scalability with little work.

Today's organizations don't operate on a single system; instead, system integration is crucial for most businesses' ability to scale. An entrepreneur can increase effectiveness by using a variety of systems.

Select the greatest technology solution for your company by consulting an IT professional.

4. Putting in place standardized procedures

Without simplified operational processes and procedures in place, scaling your organization is impossible. To make the expansion of your firm easier, you must make sure that the proper delegation of these repeatable standard operations is made.

the Indian business coach stresses the importance of aligning and standardizing the essential functions so that you can swiftly lay the groundwork for a strong foundation for the long term. You will be able to easily achieve bigger company goals by putting less emphasis on quick fixes.

5. Streamlining Procedures

By reducing your human effort, automation enables you to conduct repeated procedures seamlessly at a lesser cost and more effectively. It enables business owners to speed up the completion of any work. Additionally lowering the chance of human error, it also saves a significant amount of time. Automation, however, doesn't always include incorporating a mechanical device into the procedure and firing workers.

Automation in this context refers to the integration of a system into a process such that fewer checkpoints are required. Automation thus improves the rate (yield) at which raw goods reach their final phase in addition to quality assurance.

6. Find Your A-Team or Use Strategic Outsourcing

When it comes to growing your business, it's critical to decide when to expand your workforce or just outsource the work to a different company or independent contractors.

For instance, your core staff may include a few multitaskers in the early phases of a business. However, as the company expands, it hires specialists to enhance and optimize operations so that the core staff can focus on growing the company while maintaining quality. You must make sure that maintaining customer happiness is not in jeopardy; otherwise, you'll regret selecting the incorrect team.

7. **Recognize the needs of your clients**

Your buyer personas must be able to respond to the numerous inquiries in order to completely comprehend what your customers' true needs are.

For instance:

- Who are your clients?

- How do they purchase?

- Why are they buying?

- How do they perceive you?

- What do people anticipate of you?

Your staff will be able to comprehend what your customer actually wants thanks to these crucial points. Additionally, it's a good idea to consider your company's expansion from the standpoint of your clients. Your internal team needs to be focused and set goals for your company's success.

8. Recognize Your Competitive Advantage

It's vital to keep in mind that many business owners give in to self-perceptions of where they want their company to go when it comes to developing a competitive edge.

your marketing operations. Your customers will be impressed by the marketing initiatives you can produce.

Agile marketing framework adoption enables businesses to increase production and efficiency.

The true start of business scaling is the ideation phase. You need to know exactly where you want your company to be in 10 years. Everything will come together once you see the end of the tunnel, and scaling your business won't be as difficult as you initially anticipated.

Do not lose sight of the greater picture and the light at the end of the tunnel.

Every entrepreneur experiences a variety of difficulties along the way, but it is advisable to take precautions. You can scale your business with little to no difficulty if you have good planning, the correct staff, and a growth attitude.

Page Left Blank

CHAPTER 7

Beyond money- making an impact.

"Be somebody who make everybody feel like a somebody."

– Robby Novak

Your company does not operate in a vacuum. It is a component of your town, city, and region and is impacted by the problems that your community, city, and region are facing. You must work to bring about change outside of your company if you want to have a beneficial impact.

76% of millennials, it was discovered, check to see if a corporation is being truthful about its stance on social or environmental concerns. Many small enterprises and corporations got moving as a result. After all, millennials are extremely powerful. both as a customer and as a potential employee of a business with a track record of social responsibility.

What is Corporate Social Responsibility?

Corporate social responsibility (CSR), in its simplest form, is the practice of conducting business in a way that benefits stakeholders, employees, the environment, and society at large. The key is taking responsibility. CSR is here to stay, whether it is switching to green energy or encouraging staff to bike to work. Furthermore, CSR is gaining popularity and has been shown to advance both a company's mission and its bottom line.

Each business has a responsibility when it comes to their social influence, from large corporate businesses that sell thousands of coffees daily to a tiny business call center.

Not even small enterprises are exempt! Like anybody else, you must respond to the calls for change. Numerous businesses all around the world have been announcing their plans to address their CSR initiatives, and you ought to follow suit.

5 Reasons Why Small Businesses Should Adopt a CSR Strategy

Employers Can Be Attracted, Kept, and Engaged by CSR Strategies for Small Businesses

Employers' top concerns are almost always related to employee motivation. It takes more effort than it might appear to inspire a group of workers with a monthly salary alone. One of the most crucial factors when evaluating a job opportunity, according to 40% of young people, is a sense of purpose or influence, according to a survey of nearly 25,000 people from 186 countries between the ages of 18 and 35. And even if it meant earning less money, 55% of workers would choose to work for a company that prioritized social responsibility.

CSR programs have been shown to be successful at both maintaining your current employees and attracting the best and brightest candidates. Effective employee engagement programs help business leaders attract and retain personnel, according to 88% of business executives who responded to America's Charities' Snapshot Research poll of organizations. It makes no difference if your rival uses the top call center software that 2021 has to offer. Smaller businesses with a conscience have an advantage over their larger rivals whose CSR initiatives fall short.

Enhances Public Perception

In business, sincerity is essential. You must make sincere attempts to improve how you approach social responsibility.

Pret, a chain of organic coffee shops, is one organization that has long been committed to battling homelessness. Their nonprofit organization, "The Pret Foundation," works to reduce poverty, homelessness, and hunger. In order to give homeless people a second opportunity at life, they even actively employ them.

This is great for society and Pret's reputation. You're likely to attract the correct attention as a small business doing something beneficial for the community.

Enhances Sales

Businesses that have a strong CSR strategy see a rise in revenue. Even though this effect is frequently indirect, it nevertheless has an effect. Your company may have an advantage over a rival that has a CSR program or has one that is viewed as being unauthentic given that consumers are growing more selective about the businesses they choose to patronize. The likelihood of the buyer choosing your brand therefore increases. And if you continue to provide good customer service, you'll benefit from their return business. With live chatbots or interactive voice response (IVR), you can stay one step ahead of the competition when it comes to how they engage with clients.

Loyalty Increases

Expect increased consumer and employee loyalty when you implement a CSR strategy. As a leader, you must continually assess how your team members feel about your CSR. Also crucial to stakeholders and shareholders is having a solid understanding of social responsibility. People respect companies that work to make the world a better place. They will therefore be more likely to stick by you. They might not be interested in another company that provides the same service but does not make a CSR commitment.

Here are some strategies for making a CSR impact that will last:

Engage in charitable giving and volunteer work

When you allow your staff to pursue their passions, your business social responsibility increases. Charities in

America Snapshot Research consistently demonstrates that when you invest in your people, they invest in you and your company as well. It's a fantastic method to let someone know you care about them.

Consider the impact that your employees' health has on your company. Your commitment to corporate social responsibility might be directly related to your efforts to keep your workforce inspired and productive. Provide incentives for employees who fulfill weekly goals, such as bike-to-work plans or coupons. Give people the chance to give back to their community through workplace donations or paid time off to volunteer their skills. Such incentives are essential for achieving strong staff engagement.

Additionally, the entire company could provide its services. You may, for instance, use the assistance of your employees to donate materials to a nearby charity or give up your time for a community project. Give workers a day off and make sure they are paid. You might perform this once a month or once a year, depending on the size of your business.

Establish a CSR Department

Restructuring your business will demonstrate that you genuinely care about making a difference. Human Resources would collaborate closely with a CSR department. However, CSR would concentrate more on societal and environmental issues, while HR would have a say in issues pertaining to employees.

Additionally, SMS customer help was available for anyone who had suggestions for how your CSR could be improved from clients, staff, or other stakeholders. Additionally, by involving stakeholders in your CSR strategies, you increase your level of transparency.

Work with the Community

Another excellent option to transform your company to a CSR strategy is by supporting nonprofit organizations and forming collaborations with regional authorities. To establish a solid relationship and start your attempts to become more involved, you might begin by reaching out to community leaders. This not only raises the profile of your business but also makes it easier for locals to see the beneficial effects you are having on their neighborhood.

Additionally, you might register for sponsorship offers and fund-raising events, whether they are for the nearby town fair or a school play. For instance, the company could contribute a tiny portion of revenues to a community organization's fundraising initiative. Use bulk email tools to reach out to a large audience and see what you can learn.

CONCLUSION

We've examined the thrilling path of converting your passion into a profitable business in the book. As you finish the final chapter of "From Hobby to Money," I hope the pages have enlightened you on the possibilities that exist within your passions and fanned the flames of entrepreneurship.

Remember that the heart of this transition is not simply financial gain, but the creation of a life in which your everyday actions are motivated by genuine excitement. Your passion is more than simply a hobby; it is the foundation of your business spirit.

We've gone into the complexities of choosing the perfect passion, comprehending legal procedures, developing engaging marketing techniques, and the art of creating a dedicated team. Each step is a brushstroke on the canvas of your business, adding to the one-of-a-kind masterpiece that is yours.

Keep in mind the resilience and adaptability that every entrepreneur possesses as you embark on this new enterprise. There will be difficulties, and the route will be unpredictable, but it is in these moments that your enthusiasm will serve as a compass, directing you ahead.

Happy entrepreneuring!

Anthony White

YOUR REVIEWS ARE VERY IMPORTANT

Dear Reader,

I hope the journey through "From Hobby to Money" has been as educational for you as it has been for me. Your support means everything, and I would be eternally grateful if you would share your comments on Amazon.

Your evaluations not only provide useful input, but they also assist other prospective entrepreneurs in discovering the gems hidden inside these pages. Your thoughts, whether a sentence or a few paragraphs, have the power to inspire and encourage fellow readers on their journey from pastime to company.

To share your Amazon review, use the link below:

https://www.amazon.com/dp/B0BVGJ128Z

Or Scan the QR Code below

Thank you for being part of this exciting adventure. Your feedback is the heartbeat of the community we're building together.

Warm regards,

Anthony White

ACKNOWLEDGEMENTS

I want to thank Tess and Parker, two friends who kept encouraging me to write this essay.

I also want to thank Esther, my wife, who proofread everything and served as my accountability partner. Baby, I love you.

Last but not least, I want to thank you, the reader, for purchasing and finishing this book. Please suggest to a friend or relative.

Love,

Anthony White